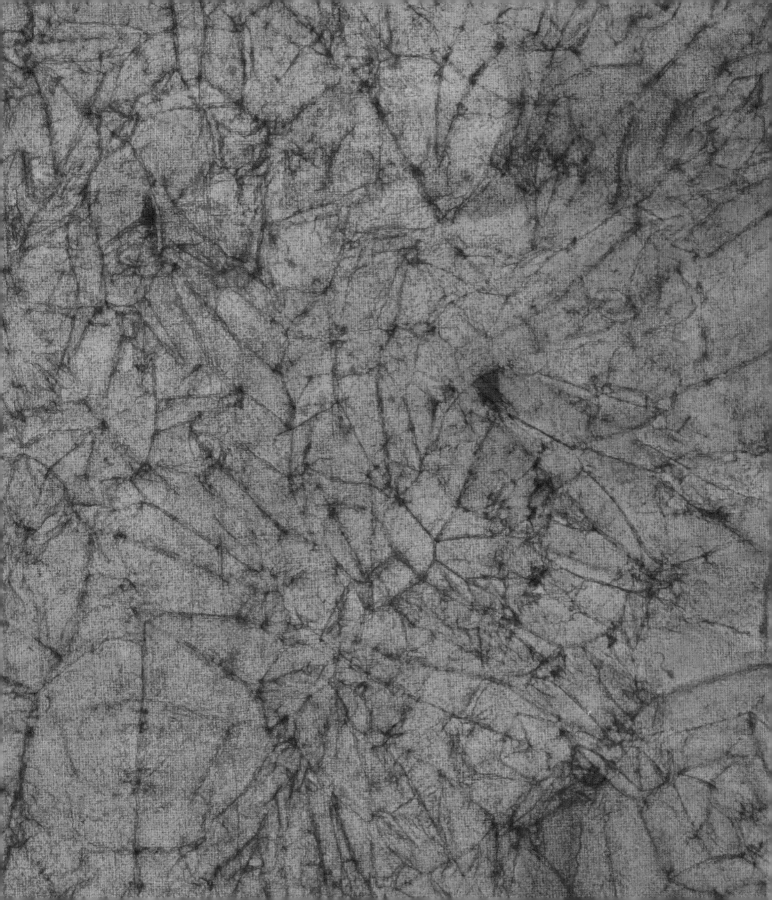

BILLIONS of YEARS, AMAZING CHANGES

LAURENCE PRINGLE

BILLIONS of YEARS, AMAZING CHANGES

THE STORY OF EVOLUTION

Illustrations by **Steve Jenkins**

With a Foreword by Jerry A. Coyne, PhD

BOYDS MILLS PRESS
Honesdale, Pennsylvania

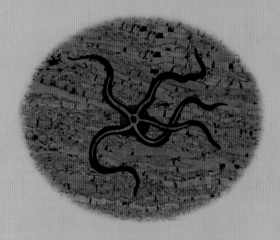

Boyds Mills Press, Inc.
815 Church Street
Honesdale, Pennsylvania 18431
Printed in China

ISBN: 978-1-59078-723-6

Library of Congress Control Number: 2011920604

First edition
The text of this book is set in 13.5-point Rotation.

10 9 8 7 6 5 4 3 2 1

Dedicated to the teachers who celebrate the ongoing adventure of science, especially those who lead their students into our deep and ever-growing understanding of evolution.

Acknowledgments

Special thanks to the John Simon Guggenheim Memorial Foundation, which in 2006 honored me with a fellowship to write about evolution for children. I also thank Kent Brown Jr. for his call in January 2009 with the happy news of a Boyds Mills Press contract for this book; the design staff, especially Robbin Gourley and Carla Weise, for their excellent work; and editor Andy Boyles for his patience, wisdom, and wit as we dealt with every tiny detail and nuance of words, photographs, and illustrations. I am deeply grateful to Dr. Jerry A. Coyne, Department of Ecology and Evolution, University of Chicago, for his careful reading of this book's manuscript. His thoroughness and detailed comments added significantly to its accuracy. Any errors that remain are mine. Finally, thanks to my wife, Susan, for her support and generosity and her continued tolerance of a writer's life, and to my staff—the cats—especially chief of staff Sabrina, for her grace and beauty, and for allowing me almost half of the seat of my office chair.

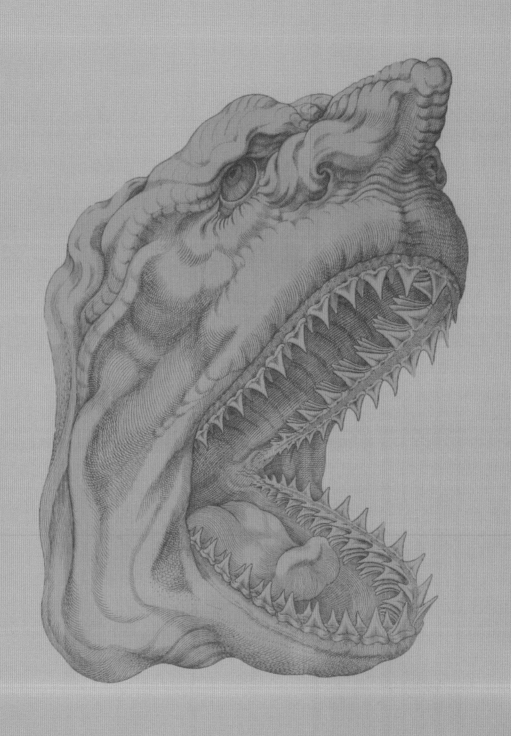

Contents

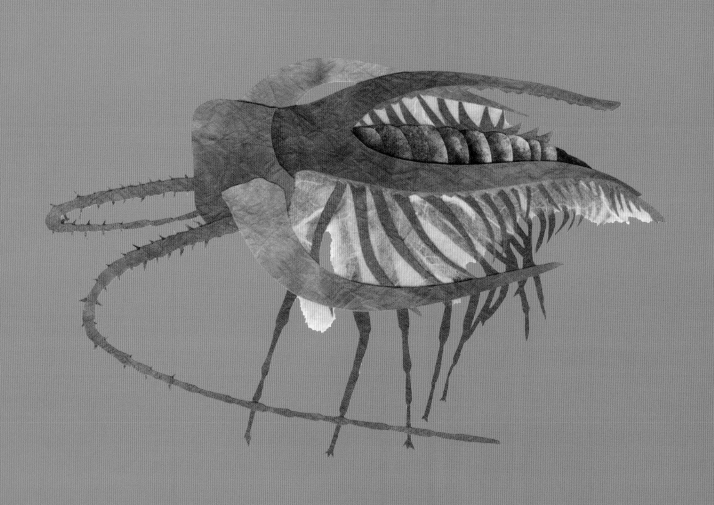

Foreword

Charles Darwin's theory of evolution by natural selection has been called "the best idea that anyone ever had." That seems about right to me. For that theory has given us the correct explanation of our origins—and by "our" I mean not just human beings, but every species that ever lived. Evolutionary biology tells us that we're related, to greater or lesser degrees, to every creature on Earth today: to monkeys and apes, to ferns, to squirrels, and even to tiny creatures that you can see only under the microscope. And evolution explains all the marvelous adaptations of animals and plants—the grasping trunk of the elephant, the sturdy beak of the woodpecker, the prickly spines of the cactus—as the results of a very simple process: natural selection.

The idea of evolution is not only one of the greatest triumphs of the human mind, but it has become the central organizing idea of biology. Whenever you look at any feature of an animal or plant, whether it involves body structure, behavior, or biochemistry, you can ask yourself: Where did it come from? How did it get there? The answer is evolution, and, usually, natural selection. As the biologist Theodosius Dobzhansky once said, "Nothing in biology makes sense except in the light of evolution."

I was exposed to a lot of science when I was young. By the time I was twelve years old I already had a big library of books about dinosaurs, geology, and all varieties of animals and plants. But I didn't have any books on evolution, because they weren't written for young people then. And although I became an evolutionary biologist, I still regret not having learned earlier how evolution ties biology together.

You are luckier, for in your hands is the book I wish I had read when I was your age. Laurence Pringle has written a wonderful account of evolution that does tie it all together. He explains the modern scientific view clearly and summarizes all of the fascinating evidence that has convinced scientists, as I hope it convinces you, that evolution is *true*. Enjoy!

JERRY A. COYNE, PhD
Professor of Ecology and Evolution
University of Chicago

 9

1

Imagine

Imagine a long time ago, in your family.

Do you remember old photographs of your great-grandparents? Perhaps you have seen an ancestor's portrait that was painted even before photography was invented.

You may have studied a family tree that gives a few details about your relatives who lived a century or more ago. It is probably hard to picture their day-to-day lives, so long ago.

For humans, both now and in the past, just a thousand years seems like a vast stretch of time. Most people who lived in the 1700s and early 1800s believed that Earth had existed for just a few thousand years. Also, they believed that the plants and animals they knew had always been the same.

A few people disagreed. They found evidence that suggested that Earth might be many millions of years old. They also learned that there had been great changes in Earth's life. The evidence was in plain sight—in the landscape and the rocks of Earth's surface.

Old family photographs remind us of past generations. It is hard for humans to imagine life stretching back for many thousands, or even millions, of years.

2

Evidence from the Earth

One of the first of all sciences was *geology*—the study of the history and structure of Earth. Some early geologists had some scientific training, but most were just curious amateurs. They liked to explore and observe different land forms, and rocks, on our planet's surface.

They could see that flowing water wore away, or *eroded*, soils and even rocks.

Clearly, a long time would be needed for water to erode hard rocks. Geologists saw that some rivers had cut through layer after rocky layer. This erosion would take huge amounts of time, much more than a few thousand years.

Geologists also found different kinds of rocks—sandstone, for example, that had once been sand but gradually became solid rock. They discovered rocks that had once been liquid—flowing lava from volcanoes. And they saw layers of rocks that were tilted and twisted by powerful forces in Earth's crust. Wherever they looked, geologists found evidence that Earth was not a few thousand years old. Instead, its surface had been changing over a mind-boggling span of time—perhaps even billions of years.

More evidence was found, in plain sight. Lying on beaches, or sticking out of rocky cliffs, or unearthed in farmers' fields, were shells, teeth, bones—made of stone. They were *fossils*.

These objects fascinated and puzzled people. What could they be? For example, what kind of animal left the big, three-toed footprints in rocks that a Massachusetts farm boy discovered in 1802? People thought that the tracks had been left by ancient birds

that they called Noah's ravens. Eventually, people learned that the footprints had been made millions of years ago by dinosaurs.

On ocean beaches, and sometimes far inland, people found stony sharp-edged triangular objects. What were they? One answer had been offered more than two thousand years ago by Pliny the Elder, a Roman scholar who studied nature. He wrote that they were stone tongues that fell to Earth from the moon. In 1667 a scientist named Nicholas Steno had a much better idea. He examined the mouth of a

The Colorado River shifted its course numerous times over a span of several million years as it eroded the wide and deep Grand Canyon.

Shark teeth are arranged in rows, one behind the other. When a tooth breaks or falls out, a new tooth moves forward to replace it. One shark can lose a thousand teeth in its lifetime, so these abundant and very hard objects are common fossils.

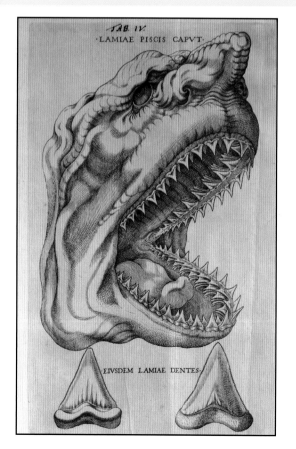

dead shark and realized that the triangular fossils were teeth of ancient sharks.

Despite the discovery of more and more fossils, many people still thought that life had never changed. They believed that no animals had completely died out, or become extinct. The third president of the United States, Thomas Jefferson, wrote that there was no evidence that nature had permitted "any race of her animals to become extinct."

Jefferson knew that remains of huge elephant-like mammoths had been dug up in Europe and North

In his 1667 drawing of a shark's head, Nicholas Steno compared a shark's tooth with a fossil tooth. He recognized that the abundant fossils were ancient shark teeth.

America. He thought that mammoths might still be alive. In the early 1800s, Jefferson sent the Lewis and Clark Expedition to explore the wild, unmapped lands west of the Mississippi River. The expedition had many goals; one was to watch out for live mammoths.

None were found. And Jefferson himself later realized that many animals had gone extinct in North America. Giant ground sloths, saber-toothed cats, and dire wolves had died out long ago. Only their fossils remained.

Explorers once hoped they would find live woolly mammoths. Now we know that the last mammoths died out about four thousand years ago.

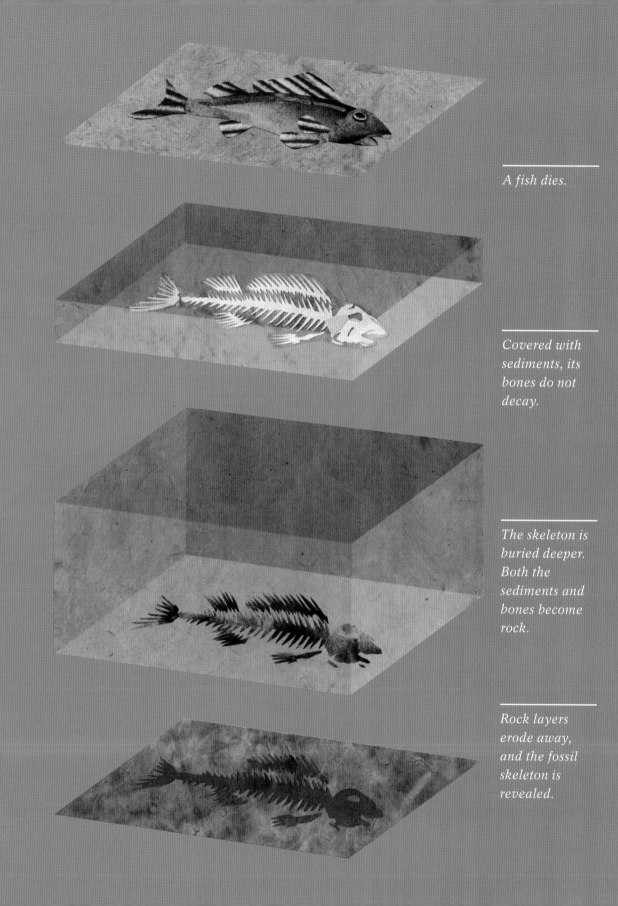

A fish dies.

Covered with sediments, its bones do not decay.

The skeleton is buried deeper. Both the sediments and bones become rock.

Rock layers erode away, and the fossil skeleton is revealed.

How Fossils Form

Most of Earth's past life leaves no trace. Soon after death, animals and plants begin to decay. Even such hard objects as bones and teeth gradually break down and disappear. Sometimes, however, a dead animal or plant is quickly covered by a sandstorm. Or, underwater, it may be buried by mud, silt, or sand. Lack of oxygen causes decay to slow, then stop. More mud or other sediments bury the animal or plant even deeper. Eventually, pressure from the weight of even more sediments above causes both the mud and the once-living objects in it to turn to rock. Calcium and other elements that make up bones are slowly replaced by minerals. What was once a tree trunk, a seashell, or a fish skeleton gradually becomes a stony replica of itself.

Sometimes just a detailed imprint of an animal or plant is left in the rocks. Animal footprints—

These dinosaur footprints, preserved in sandstone, were uncovered in Connecticut in 1966. They are about two hundred million years old.

including those of dinosaurs—have also been preserved in stone. So have animal droppings!

The rarest fossils of all are soft things, such as leaves, and such delicate creatures as insects and spiders. Nevertheless, under the right conditions they become fossils. One way is for small creatures to be trapped in a sticky fluid called resin that oozes from certain kinds of trees. Over many, many years, some globs of resin change into rocklike, clear amber—with ancient life preserved within.

The process of fossilization continues today. Insects are still caught in tree resin. Dead animals are still covered with sand, mud, or silt on the bottoms of oceans, seas, lakes, and river deltas. Layers of slate and other rocks—and fossils preserved in them—are forming. All over Earth, some examples of life today will gradually become fossils that might be discovered in a far-distant tomorrow.

Layers of Rock, Layers of Past Life

Study of Earth's rocks, and fossils in them, has led to startling discoveries and puzzling questions. A scholar in ancient Greece, Xenophanes, was among the first to write of finding fish fossils in the rocks of high mountain ranges. He concluded that those lands had once been underwater.

This idea was rejected when Xenophanes lived, about 2,500 years ago. It became more widely accepted in the early 1500s, thanks to the writings of Leonardo da Vinci, a great painter, engineer, and scientist of those times. He had found fossils of marine (saltwater)

Fossils of saltwater fish are often found far from today's oceans.

Layers of sedimentary rocks can often be seen in canyon walls or along roadsides. The upper layers formed more recently than those below.

animals in the mountains of northern Italy. This was more evidence that an ocean or sea had once covered the area. Underwater, layers of rocks—with fossils in them—had formed and later had been pushed up, far into the air. Although people had experienced earthquakes, it was hard for them to imagine even greater changes in Earth's crust, but the evidence was there—in fossils of sea life hundreds of miles from ocean coasts.

Geologists also noticed differences in layers, or *strata*, of *sedimentary* rocks.

These are the most common rocks of Earth's surface. They include siltstone, shale, and sandstone. Beginning in the 1600s, geologists concluded that the topmost rock layers were the youngest. Layers just below were older, and strata farther down were older still.

Around 1800 an Englishman, William Smith, noticed something remarkable about different rock layers. He was an engineer involved in digging canals. This work often uncovered several strata of sedimentary rocks. Smith found different kinds of fossils in different rock layers. Some French geologists noticed this, too. And when they compared the fossils from different rock layers, they saw a clear pattern.

The fossils from the youngest rocks—those closest to the surface—were similar to living animals—mammals, reptiles, and fish. These kinds of fossils did not exist in the deeper layers of rocks. In much older rocks, geologists found mollusk shells, vast numbers of extinct

Scientists saw that deeper and much older layers of rock contained fossils of more simple forms of life (for example, no animals with backbones).

21

Five hundred million years ago, trilobites were abundant ocean animals with hard protective shells. Today they are common fossils in sedimentary rocks.

creatures called trilobites, and other animals without backbones. The rock layers and their fossils showed that both Earth and its life had undergone amazing changes over an unimaginable span of time.

Fossil skeleton of the earliest known hoofed mammal, sixty million years ago (on display at the Smithsonian Natural History Museum).

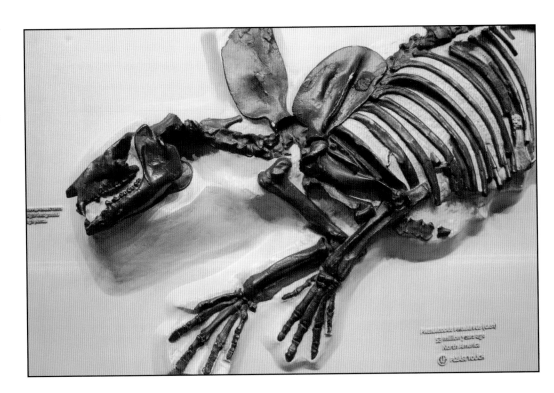

5

The Adventures and Discoveries of Charles Darwin

Despite the growing evidence of an ancient Earth, some people still believed that our planet was quite young. They thought that a great flood, or perhaps several floods, had swept the entire planet. These catastrophes had carried marine life inland. For some people, this explained the presence of marine fossils far from oceans.

All over the world, however, geologists found more evidence of a very different explanation. In 1830, British geologist Charles Lyell wrote a book about Earth's history, called *Principles of Geology.*

The eruption of volcanoes created the Galápagos, including Bartolome Island. It is one of the younger islands, so plants do not yet cover the lava landscape.

While he was a schoolboy, Charles Darwin read a book called *The Hundred Wonders of the World*, which made him eager to explore faraway places. Charles loved to collect things: coins, seashells, minerals, insects. When he was a nineteen-year-old student at Cambridge University, he competed with friends: who could collect the greatest variety of insects? He wrote, "One day . . . I saw two rare beetles, and seized one in each hand; then I saw a third and new kind, which I could not bear to lose, so I popped the one which I held in my right hand into my mouth. Alas! He ejected some intensely acrid fluid, which burnt my tongue so that I was forced to spit the beetle out, which was lost, as was the third one."

He challenged the notion that Earth was young. Lyell described geological change that people could witness in their lifetimes: earthquakes lifting land, volcanoes creating islands, erosion at work everywhere. Given plenty of time, these natural happenings, occurring all over Earth's surface, could have caused great changes.

Lyell's *Principles of Geology* was aboard a British ship, HMS *Beagle*, which set out in December 1831 on a voyage of exploration. (Planned for two years, the mission took five.) Lyell's book was brought by Charles Darwin, a young naturalist on the voyage. Darwin was fascinated by Lyell's ideas and soon witnessed powerful forces at work on Earth's crust. He saw a volcano erupt and felt a mighty earthquake. He saw a city— Concepción, Chile—destroyed by that earthquake.

Along the coast of South America, Charles Darwin and the ship's captain and crew saw other changes caused by the earthquake. Large areas that had been underwater had been lifted into the air. Exploring inland, 7,000 feet (about 2,100 meters) above sea level, the men found fossil seashells in the rocks. Darwin realized that the Andes mountain chain, with some peaks 14,000 feet (about 4,300 meters) above sea level, was probably created by mighty forces in Earth's crust.

Wherever the *Beagle* anchored near land, Darwin explored and wrote his observations in journals. He collected specimens of plants and animals. He also found fossils of elephant-size ground sloths and other animals that had gone extinct.

In 1835, the *Beagle* spent five weeks among the Galápagos, a cluster of islands six hundred miles (nearly one thousand kilometers) off the coast of South America. All of the islands had formed from volcanic lava and ash. All had arisen from underwater volcanoes and had no life on them when they first appeared. Some were ancient, eroded remains of volcanoes; others had formed during more recent eruptions. Nature had created the Galápagos over several million years. Because of their different ages, the islands had different living conditions, or habitats. For example, only a few plants grew on recent flows of lava. Rich tropical forests grew on older islands, where soils had gradually formed. On the Galápagos Islands, Darwin also discovered an amazing variety of unusual animals. They included birds called cormorants that could not fly, iguanas that swam for food beneath the ocean waves, and giant

Marine iguanas of the Galápagos live on rocky coasts and dive underwater to feed on algae.

The large cactus finch lives on just four of the Galápagos Islands.

tortoises. (In Spanish, *galápago* means "the front part of a riding saddle." The tortoise shells resemble saddles.)

Many of the Galápagos animals lived nowhere else on Earth. And they also differed from island to island. For example, Darwin found three kinds (*species*) of mockingbirds, each living on a different island. He collected specimens of mockingbirds, other birds, and other animal and plant life. After the *Beagle* visited New Zealand, Australia, and parts of the African coast, it returned to England in 1836.

Scientists eagerly studied the biological treasures that Darwin brought home. An expert on birds (*ornithologist*) examined the skins (with beaks and feathers) that Darwin had preserved. Darwin had identified some of the birds as wrens, blackbirds, or finches. He thought one was a grosbeak—a kind of bird known for having a big beak. However, the ornithologist discovered that many of these birds—including the so-called grosbeak—were *all* finches.

Around the world, most finch species have small beaks, well suited for eating small seeds. The Galápagos finches were different. Some had sharp-pointed beaks, useful for catching insects. Others had big beaks for crushing big seeds. There was even a finch species whose beak and behavior were like those of a woodpecker.

Charles Darwin had an idea of how this surprising variety of finches lived on the Galápagos. He wrote that "one might really fancy" that the variety of finches began when just one species somehow reached the Galápagos. Other scientists reasoned that a powerful storm had carried a few finches from Ecuador to some of the Galápagos Islands. Then, over a long span of time, that one species of finch changed until fourteen new finch species lived on different islands. Darwin wondered how these changes had happened.

Common Cactus Finch

Large Ground Finch   *Woodpecker Finch*   *Vegetarian Finch*   *Warbler Finch*

A variety of finches evolved from one species that reached the Galápagos. The finches vary in size, and especially in the size and shape of their beaks.

6

Evolution

Evolution is, simply, change over time. It usually means a gradual change, not a quick one. People use the term about all sorts of things. They might say a sports team evolved from being a perennial loser into a champion.

Life on Earth has evolved. This idea was not new with Charles Darwin. Scholars in ancient Greece believed that life had developed gradually, changing from simple to more complex organisms. This idea began to take hold again in the eighteenth century. Darwin's own grandfather, Erasmus Darwin, offered evidence of changes in animals "gradually produced over many generations."

A huge question remained: how did these changes actually happen? One answer was proposed in 1800 by French scientist Jean-Baptiste Lamarck. He wrote that all animals contained a "nervous fluid" that made changes happen. For example, when a giraffe stretched its neck to reach food, nervous fluid flowed to its neck. This caused the neck to grow longer. When the giraffe mated and produced baby giraffes, their necks would be longer, too.

This made no sense to other scientists who studied living animals or the fossils of extinct ones. There was no evidence that nervous fluid existed. And, more important, no one saw animals changing quickly, with noticeable physical changes in just a few generations. Lamarck's ideas were rejected.

Scientists continued to wonder how evolution "worked." As it

Giraffes evolved very long necks, but not in the way suggested by Lamarck.

In 1858 Alfred Russel Wallace explained, in a brief report, the basic idea of how evolution worked. By that time, however, Darwin had nearly finished writing a long, detailed book about the same idea. When Wallace read Darwin's *On the Origin of Species*, he wrote, "Mr. Darwin has given the world a new science, and his name should, in my opinion, stand above that of every philosopher of ancient or modern times."

turned out, in the 1840s and 1850s, two men were edging closer to the answer. One was Charles Darwin. After the voyage of the *Beagle*, he continued to study the animals and plants he had collected. He also did research on pigeons, barnacles, and coral reefs. He wrote scientific articles and books on these and other subjects. By the mid-1800s, Darwin was one of the most respected scientists in England (and, for that matter, in the whole world). By 1858, after twenty years of investigation and thinking, Darwin had nearly finished writing a book that explained how evolution worked.

In another part of the world, another scientist's discoveries and thinking led him to the same explanation. Like Darwin, Alfred Russel Wallace had explored far from England. He had observed nature and collected animals in the Amazon region of South America and in the Malay Archipelago (now Indonesia).

On June 18, 1858, Darwin received a letter from Wallace that explained his ideas about evolution. Independently, both men had figured out how life on Earth changes.

Wallace's letter prompted Darwin to finish the book he had been preparing for many years. *On the Origin of Species* was published in the fall of 1859.

Although both men had the same basic idea, today few people know about Wallace. Charles Darwin became famous. And, though he died in 1882, his ideas live on.

They changed human understanding of all life on Earth.

Charles Darwin worked hard to answer questions that might be asked about his explanations of evolution. He thought deeply and broadly about every detail. Darwin revised *On the Origin of Species* five times, added new information, and rewrote more than three quarters of his sentences. This made the book even stronger.

7

Variation

The process of evolution depends on four basic characteristics of nature.

One is variation, which means there is great variety among living things—including among members of the same kind, or species. We see this variety in our everyday lives. Think of the variety of people you see. Or, if you have had pet cats, dogs, or other animals, think of how they differ. Domestic cats are all one species—*Felis catus*. Each cat shares many characteristics with every other cat, but they also differ in some ways. The same is true of dogs. Individuals of one species, *Canis familiaris*, vary a great deal in their size, behavior, hair length, and other features.

Dogs vary greatly in size and appearance, yet are all one species.

There is variation in all of nature, even in a school of striped catfish (top) that may look identical, or in a nesting colony of gannets (bottom) on the coast of North Island, New Zealand.

It is easy to see variation in people or cats or dogs. Variation is less visible when we see a photo of a huge school of fish or a meadow of flowers. They may all look alike, but variation is there. It is everywhere in nature. It makes evolution possible.

Both Charles Darwin and his grandfather Erasmus were curious about variation in nature. They knew that farmers used knowledge of this variation when they chose certain animals to breed. Charles Darwin asked questions of people who bred cattle, dogs, pigeons, sheep, and goldfish. He raised and studied pigeons himself. (At one point, he kept nearly ninety birds.)

Some dairy farmers had learned how to get more milk from their cow herds. For breeding, they picked cows that gave the most milk. Those cows usually produced young that also became good milk producers. By continuing to pick certain cows for breeding, eventually a farmer could have a whole herd of cows that gave more milk than average.

Plant growers also crossbred certain flower, vegetable, and fruit plants. By doing so they could produce, for example, a rosebush with a new blossom color. Or, they could select certain tomato plants for breeding and develop a variety that had fast-ripening fruit. Clearly, by selecting individual plants and animals for breeding, people could change future generations. They did this by deliberately picking certain individuals for breeding.

Charles Darwin explained how a natural process could change all life on Earth—not just livestock, flowers, and other organisms picked by humans. The variation among individuals present in all living species makes this possible.

8

Nature's Bounty

Nature is bountiful. One female salmon can produce twenty-eight million eggs, each one a potential adult fish. A pair of rats can produce as many as two thousand descendants in a year, if all their young survive and also begin to reproduce. Plants also have a great capacity for increasing their numbers. Just one dandelion flower can produce seeds for more than a hundred new plants. From a single oak tree, thousands of acorns fall to the forest floor. Each one has the potential of becoming a towering tree.

Populations of animals and plants have a tremendous capacity for growth. This great bounty of nature is a second key factor in evolution. If all eggs, seeds, and young survived to become adults that also reproduced, the world would soon be overrun with living things. There isn't enough space, food, or other resources to allow all to survive.

The result is another key factor in the process of evolution: *competition*.

Just one flower (right) yields seeds for scores of new dandelion plants. Each sprouting acorn (left) is a potential tree.

9

Competition

Gardeners sometimes walk along rows of young plants, pulling out seedlings. Often more than half of the young plants are tossed aside and die. They are removed so the remaining plants have enough space and sunlight in which to grow to full size.

In the wild, a similar process occurs naturally. Many plants and animals die, and this allows others to develop, thrive, and produce a new generation. Some animals die by having accidents, as when a bird flying across a road is hit by a car. Many animals and plants die when they lose in competition with others of their kind. Underground, the roots of tree saplings compete for water and minerals. Aboveground, the saplings compete for sunlight and growing space. Competition is the third factor in the process of evolution.

In a coral reef, some kinds of fish compete for good hiding places. They feed close to the reef and dash for shelter when a shark or a school of jacks appears. Fish that are not alert or are too slow or are unable to find a hiding place are usually the first to die. These fish do not mate and do not pass their characteristics to the next generation.

Birds also compete—for food, mates, and nesting places. Male birds sing to attract a mate and to defend a territory that includes one or more nesting sites. Some males lose in the competition entirely. No females choose them, so they do not mate and reproduce.

Throughout nature, many organisms fail to survive and reproduce. Others mate and produce a new generation. This

situation is somewhat like a farmer who picks certain cattle to breed. We call the farmer's choices artificial selection. In nature, however, no one decides which animals and plants survive to mate. This happens naturally, through a process that is the fourth vital factor of evolution: *natural selection*.

Competing for food and hiding places in a coral reef, some fishes survive and others do not. Only the survivors can pass their characteristics on to a new generation when they reproduce.

Natural Selection

In the spring, when male and female wood frogs hop away from ponds, they leave masses of hundreds of fertilized eggs in the water. Soon tadpoles (sometimes called pollywogs) hatch from the eggs. The tiny tadpoles swim by swinging their tails from side to side. They begin to eat and grow. And some die. Tadpoles are eaten by birds, water beetles, dragonfly nymphs, and other predators.

Surviving tadpoles are still alive because they are quick swimmers or are good at hiding. They develop into young frogs. Then they leave the water and spread out into the woods. In this habitat, too, danger lurks. Raccoons, snakes, and birds eat wood frogs. The frogs also face the challenge of catching insects and other foods. By the fall, their numbers have dwindled. The surviving frogs are those that did best—first as tadpoles, then as adults on land.

As autumn nights grow more chilly, the wood frogs search for hiding places on the forest floor. They go into a deep sleep. Only the most fit survive to emerge in the spring. They hop toward ponds, where the winter ice has just melted. The males begin to call. Their nighttime clacking sounds are often the first frog calls of the spring.

Female wood frogs listen. They choose to mate with certain males. Something about these males—perhaps the strength of their calls—makes them more appealing to females. Some males lose in

Nature produces many wood-frog tadpoles (left), but predators reduce their numbers. On land, some adult frogs (center) also die. Only a few survive to reproduce and pass their characteristics on to a new generation (right).

this competition and do not mate. Only certain males and females mate and pass their characteristics on to the next generation. They are well *adapted* to survive in the land and water environment of wood frogs. They survive to reproduce—not by chance, but in a natural process. It is called natural selection.

In 1864, the English philosopher Herbert Spencer called natural selection "survival of the fittest," but this expression misses a key idea. A frog or a wolf or a butterfly can be very successful in its environment—"the fittest"—but it must mate successfully for its *traits* to be passed on to a new generation. An animal or plant that fails to reproduce loses its chance to affect the future of its population. Reproduction, not just survival, is the key to natural selection.

After Darwin

Darwin's *On the Origin of Species* was a best seller. The book's first printing sold out in one day! In 1859 it caused scientists all over the world to think in new ways about how Earth's life had changed. It continues to do so. Today *Origin of Species*, as it is often called, is considered the most important book in the history of science.

And today some people call evolution "Darwinism." If Charles Darwin were alive, this would please him but might also annoy him. He was a very good scientist and knew that scientific discoveries always lead to new questions. His own research did not end with publication of *Origin of Species*. He continued to observe, investigate, and think carefully. He wrote ten more books. He was

Thomas Huxley was a scientist who praised the "solid and broad bridge of facts" in Darwin's *Origin of Species*. After reading Darwin's explanation of evolution by natural selection, Huxley wrote, "How extremely stupid not to have thought of that!"

pleased to know that many scientists were studying questions that his books raised.

Today Darwin would be delighted to learn how his ideas about evolution have stood the test of time. He would also be quick to give credit to countless thousands of scientists who have studied geology, fossils, and living organisms. More than 150 years have passed since *Origin of Species* was published. Most of what we understand about the process of evolution was discovered in that time. Scientists now have ways of studying Earth and its life that did not exist in Darwin's time. Some of their amazing discoveries are described in the following chapters.

Scientists sometimes refer to the "theory of evolution," and this phrase confuses some people. There is so much evidence about evolution, and how it works, why call it "just" a theory? After all, in everyday conversation, *theory* usually means an idea, a hunch, a rough guess. However, in science, *theory* means something dramatically different. It is a well-understood set of ideas, supported by a tremendous amount of research and findings.

Scientists use the word *theory* the way people in everyday conversation use *fact*. However, by strict scientific definition, theories never become facts. Theories *explain* facts. There are other scientific theories, such as the theory of gravity, which explains why things fall when we drop them. It is very well understood, but is still called a scientific theory. Also, just a few centuries ago, people believed that many diseases were caused by curses or by evil spirits or by breathing night air. Today we have the germ theory of infectious disease, which explains that those diseases are caused by microbes. No scientist would ever say that the theories of gravity, germs, or evolution are "just" theories. That would be nonsense, because they know that theories—the scientific kind— are backed by huge amounts of trustworthy evidence.

Telling Time

Trilobites, dinosaurs, giant megalodon sharks, woolly mammoths—these are just a few kinds of animals that thrived long ago and are now extinct. *When* they lived, and for how long, was once a great mystery. Now scientists have several ways of figuring out the age of ancient rocks and the fossils in or near them.

Since 1945, scientists have been able to measure the age of some kinds of rocks, stretching back millions—even billions—of years. Many parts of Earth's crust contain *igneous* rocks, which are hardened lava and ash from volcanoes. Igneous rocks contain

Lava from volcanoes cools and hardens to form igneous rock.

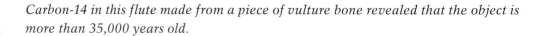

elements that are *radioactive*. This means they are unstable. They emit particles and energy at a fairly constant rate. This process is called *radioactive decay*. Eventually, after huge amounts of time, the radioactivity is all gone.

Different radioactive elements decay at different rates. This is expressed as an element's half-life—the time needed for half of its radioactivity to disappear. Geologists can accurately find out how much radioactivity was originally in igneous rocks when they formed. Comparing that amount with how much remains at this time gives a good estimate of the age of the rock. So the decay of radioactive elements in rocks can be used as a kind of natural clock.

Scientists use the element uranium-238 to figure out the age of very old rocks. U-238 decays very slowly. It has a half-life of about 700 million years. Other elements, such as potassium-40, have even longer half-lives. On the other hand, carbon-14 has a short half-life of 5,730 years. It requires the presence of some once-living materials, such as bone or wood. It has been used to determine the ages of rocks, fossils, remains of mammoths, and even old paintings and fabrics—anything in the range of 100 to 50,000 years. In 2009, measurements of carbon-14 helped archeologists learn the age of a flute uncovered in a German cave. It had been crafted from a hollow bone of a vulture more than 35,000 years ago.

Measuring radioactivity that remains in rocks does not give exact ages, but errors are usually small. For example, igneous rocks from a Canadian volcanic ash bed were judged to be 72.5 million years old *plus or minus* 0.2 million years. The possible error is less than one percent. (Only one method of dating gives exact numbers: counting the annual growth rings of trees. Remains of oak trees from Irish bogs have been dated back 7,468 years.)

Carbon-14 in this flute made from a piece of vulture bone revealed that the object is more than 35,000 years old.

Annual growth rings show that some bristlecone pines have lived nearly five thousand years in the western United States.

Radioactive measurements tell the ages of igneous rocks, but fossils are usually found in sedimentary rocks. This means that radioactivity usually cannot be used to tell the age of fossils directly. However, igneous rocks are often found between layers of sedimentary rocks. By knowing the ages of the igneous rocks, scientists can figure out the ages of adjoining sedimentary rocks and the fossils in them.

New sources of information about ancient time are being discovered and tested. Radioactivity stored in coral from ancient reefs is proving to be useful. Scientists expect that human ability to tell the age of Earth's crust and fossils will get even better.

13

Genetics

You have probably heard of *DNA*. Television crime dramas often refer to DNA as key evidence that helps identify a criminal. DNA is in the news a lot. Sometimes DNA evidence helps free a person who was wrongly convicted of a crime.

Saying these important letters—DNA—would have caused puzzled looks back in Darwin's time—or even a century ago. People knew that crossbreeding animals and plants led to offspring that had characteristics of both parents. This could produce a faster racehorse, a new breed of dog, a new tulip color. And Charles Darwin had explained how a natural selection process could also produce change. But exactly how this happened was a great mystery.

Where did the variation in the features of animals and plants come from, and how did it affect new generations? Part of the answer came from the work of Gregor Mendel, a monk and plant scientist (*botanist*) in Austria. He crossbred sweet peas, producing plants of different heights and blossom colors. He discovered the basic idea of genetics—the science of how traits and characteristics are inherited.

Mendel published his findings, but he died in 1884 without anyone realizing the importance of his research. His ideas were discovered around the year 1900—the beginning of the twentieth century. In that century scientists made great breakthroughs in our understanding of genetics.

Now we know that the *nucleus*, or center, of cells contains large DNA molecules. (*DNA* stands for *deoxyribonucleic acid*.)

Different parts of DNA, called genes, carry the genetic information of each living thing—like a set of instructions. When animals mate or a plant flower is pollinated, these instructions are blended to produce a new individual having copies of genes from both parents. However, DNA molecules are sometimes damaged, which can lead to changes in the instructions. Also, when cells divide there can be mistakes in copying the complex DNA molecules. Such changes in DNA are called *mutations*.

Mutations can be minor—so trivial that they cause no good or bad effect on a newborn animal or newly formed plant seeds. However, sometimes a mutation can have a big, harmful effect—for example, if it produces a baby snake lacking normal color (an albino). The snake can be kept alive in a zoo, but in the wild it would be easily seen by predators and probably would not survive for long. On the other hand, if a mutation caused a newborn snake to have a better-than-average sense of smell, the snake would benefit. It would be likely to survive, mate, and pass its good scent-detecting trait on to a new generation. Eventually, after many generations, this trait might be widespread through a whole population of snakes.

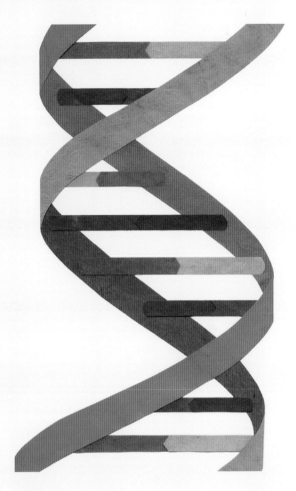

During the 1940s, scientists learned that the chemical called DNA carried genetic information from one generation to the next. But the structure of DNA molecules and how they worked were mysteries. In 1953, James Watson and Francis Crick solved these mysteries. They learned that DNA is a *double helix*—a pair of twisted strands (above). The discoveries of Watson and Crick, and of many others who study genetics, have led to a much better understanding of evolution.

Katydids are normally well camouflaged. When a mutation produces a pink katydid, the insect can easily be seen by a bird or other predator.

Remember, variation among individuals of a species is a key factor in the process of evolution. Now we know that changes in DNA cause mutations, and these mutations help produce variation in living things.

The science of genetics is producing more and more evidence of how life evolves. It has already changed ideas about how closely some animals are related to others. Usually biologists compare skeletons, organs, and other physical features to help figure out which creatures are close relatives. Now they can compare the DNA of different creatures. Generally, DNA comparisons confirm what scientists had concluded by comparing bones and other physical features. Sometimes there are surprises—for example, the discovery that parrots, falcons, and chickadees are closely related. You would not think so based on the looks or behavior of these birds, but their DNA tells a different story.

Genetic information is now a powerful tool in the study of evolution. One exciting discovery involved finches of the Galápagos—

the birds that Darwin studied. Scientists studied the DNA of finch species living on the islands and found that every one had a single common ancestor that lived in South America. So, modern DNA research proved that Darwin was correct in his thinking about the origin of all the Galápagos finches.

A complete set of genetic information in cells of each living thing is called its *genome*. A genome can be thought of as a code or a blueprint—a set of directions for "building" a new individual. In 2003, scientists were able to read all of the information encoded in the DNA of a human genome. (Dozens more have since been analyzed.) The genomes of other organisms have also been deciphered—including those of rice plants, bacteria, mice, birds, dogs, mosquitoes, the Tasmanian devil, the duck-billed platypus (an

Tiny fruit flies have played a big role in genetic research. In laboratories, they are easy to raise in large numbers. Females lay up to a hundred eggs a day. Fruit flies have a variety of eye colors and other features that make them ideal subjects for experiments in crossbreeding. The fruit fly genome was deciphered in the year 2000, and these insects continue to help humans understand evolution.

unusual egg-laying mammal), and the cacao tree, whose seeds are the source of chocolate.

Identifying the specific DNA parts of an animal or plant cell is no easy task. Decoding the genome of a single female platypus from Australia required the work of a hundred scientists in eight countries. They found that the platypus—named Glennie—had about 18,500 genes. That's about two-thirds the number of the human genome. About eighty percent of platypus genes were the same as those found in humans, dogs, mice, and opossums. (The genes may be the same, but they are arranged in different ways in different species.)

DNA studies have led to a new understanding of how animals

develop. A whole new kind of research has opened up. It is called evolutionary developmental biology, or *evo-devo*. By using knowledge of DNA, researchers can learn how certain genes affect an animal's development. They have discovered that some genes have great powers. These are called control, or *toolkit*, genes. For example, genes in the *Pax6* group control the development of eyes in animals as different as mice and humans. A gene called *BMP4* affects development of bones and beaks. One called *Distal-less* starts growth of all sorts of legs and arms—of starfish, lobsters, butterflies, cats. Another, called *CaM*, affects the length of a bird's beak. When extra amounts of this gene were put into chicken embryos, they developed longer-than-normal beaks.

These discoveries show that entire genomes do not need to change for evolution to occur. Changes in a few key genes can have big effects on new generations.

Our understanding of genetics has solved many mysteries about evolution. Think back to the animal and plant breeders who chose certain individuals for mating. They aimed to produce desirable traits in a new generation. They were pleased to have faster racehorses or a different-colored flower, but did not understand why these results occurred. Think also of Charles Darwin and other scientists who studied natural selection and the origin of new species. They, too, did not understand how evolution "worked."

Now we know that there is genetic variation in all plants and animals. We know that mutations in DNA are part of that variation. We know that each new generation can bring genetic change—the basis for evolution. As humans learn even more about genetics, they will also learn more about how living things evolve.

14

More and More Fossils

In the long history of life on Earth, most species of animals have gone extinct. Some flourished for millions of years, but they're long gone. Sometimes only a few fragments of these once-living creatures remain at or close to the surface, where people can find them. But these fossils do exist, and many are being found. By comparing fossil bones and teeth with parts of living animals, scientists can learn a lot about the lives of long-extinct animals. Scientists who study Earth's past life are called *paleontologists.*

When fossils of both animals and plants are found in the same layers of rocks, they give clues to long-ago environments. For example, fossils from Antarctica reveal that its climate was once much warmer. Now that continent is the coldest place on Earth, where ice sheets hide most of the fossil-bearing rocks. Nevertheless, in exposed rock strata scientists have found fossils of several kinds of dinosaurs. One meat-eating dinosaur, whose skeleton was nearly complete, measured 26 feet (8 meters) tall. Discovery of fossil leaves and wood is evidence that lush forests also grew on Antarctica more than two hundred million years ago.

Among the amazing fossils from all over the world are many giant animals. The skull and bones of a 42-foot-long (13 meters) snake were uncovered in an open-pit coal mine in Colombia. A fossil skeleton found in Uruguay belonged to a giant rat. Scientists estimate that this animal was the size of a rhinoceros. It was Earth's largest rodent, and lived about four million years ago.

Much longer ago, in the time of dinosaurs, flying reptiles called

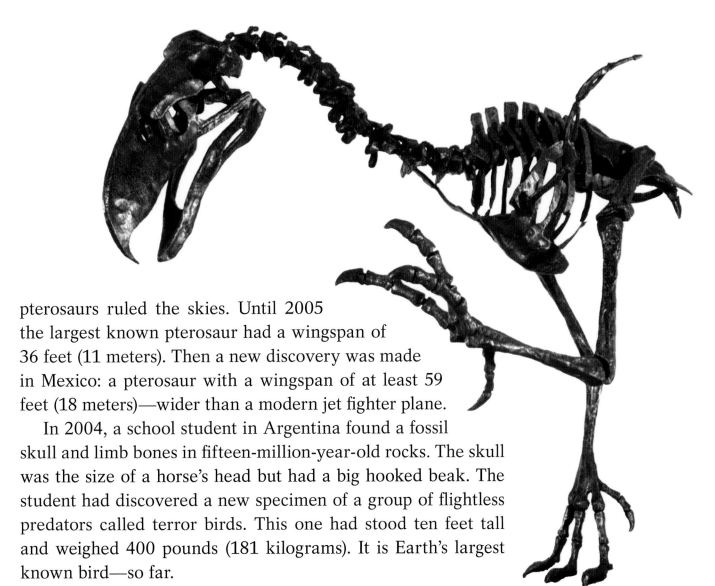

pterosaurs ruled the skies. Until 2005 the largest known pterosaur had a wingspan of 36 feet (11 meters). Then a new discovery was made in Mexico: a pterosaur with a wingspan of at least 59 feet (18 meters)—wider than a modern jet fighter plane.

In 2004, a school student in Argentina found a fossil skull and limb bones in fifteen-million-year-old rocks. The skull was the size of a horse's head but had a big hooked beak. The student had discovered a new specimen of a group of flightless predators called terror birds. This one had stood ten feet tall and weighed 400 pounds (181 kilograms). It is Earth's largest known bird—so far.

Of course, not all fossils are of extinct giants. In 2009, Canadian researchers announced that they had found fossils of one of North America's *smallest* meat-eating dinosaurs. It lived in swamps and forests seventy-five million years ago. It had sharp-toothed jaws and probably looked like a skinny, mostly featherless, but dangerous, chicken.

One of the most extraordinary fossil discoveries of all came from sedimentary rocks in British Columbia. The rocks are called the Burgess Shale. The name alone excites paleontologists.

Flightless terror birds were major predators in South America for sixty million years. Fossils of a North American species have been found in Florida and Texas.

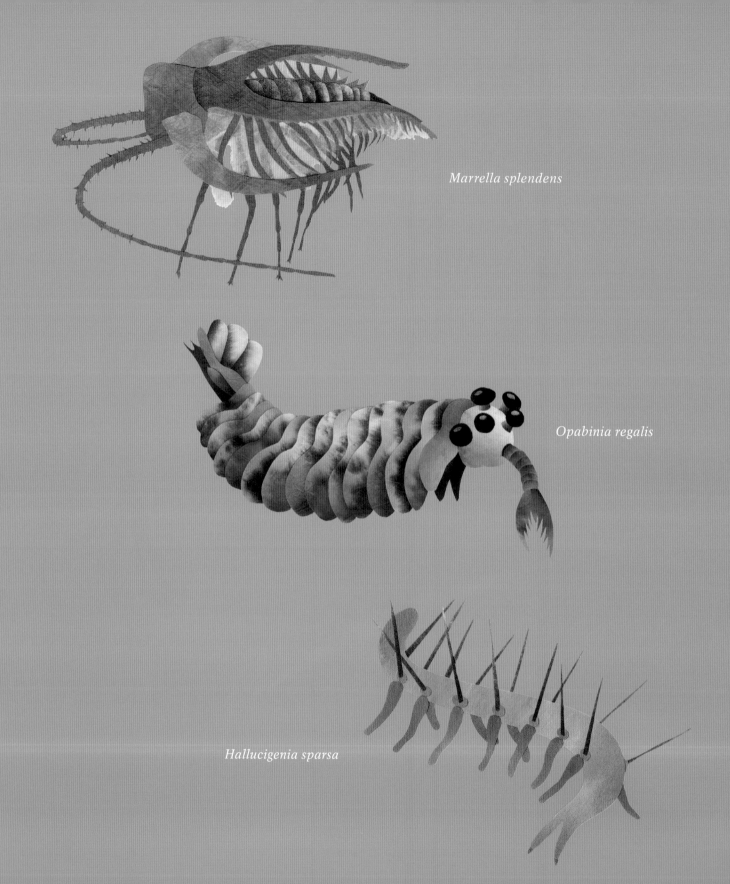

Marrella splendens

Opabinia regalis

Hallucigenia sparsa

The Burgess Shale of British Columbia contains fossils of unusual ancient soft-bodied sea creatures. Three, with their scientific names, are shown to the left.

Numerous books and museum exhibits have been inspired by creatures fossilized about 515 million years ago in the Burgess Shale. Apparently a giant mud slide swiftly buried thousands of sea creatures. They were covered so quickly and deeply that there was almost no decay. Even soft-bodied creatures became fossilized.

This treasure trove of fossils from the Burgess Shale has helped scientists picture life on a seafloor a half billion years ago.

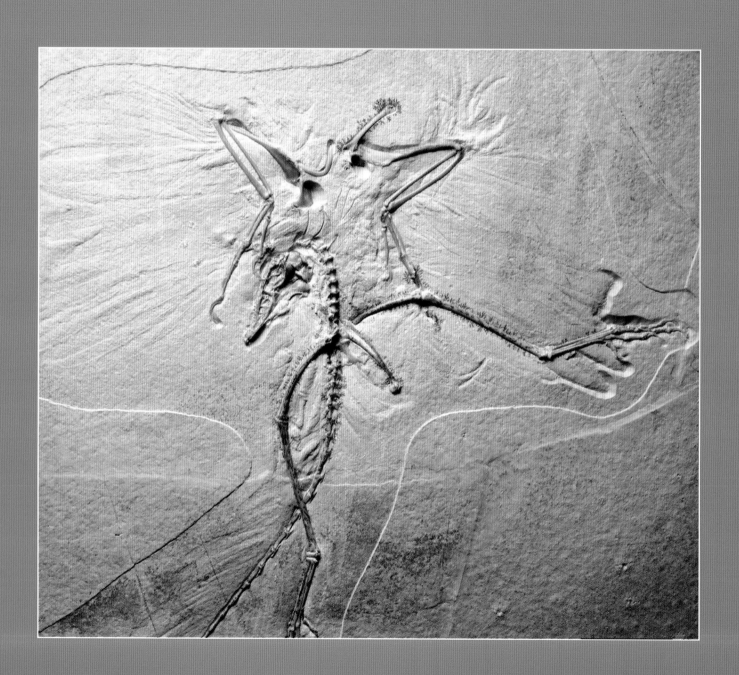

15

"Missing Links," Found

Whether a fossil is an insect in amber, a trail of dinosaur footprints, or an imprint of a leaf, it gives information about Earth's past life and about how life evolved. Since evolution means genetic change over time, people are especially curious about how one kind of living thing evolves into another. They hope to find fossils of in-between stages, which they call transitional forms. These have also been called "missing links."

Some of the most exciting news about evolution today is that more and more of these "missing links" are no longer missing. One example comes from the evolution of birds from dinosaurs—an idea suggested by Thomas Huxley, a friend of Charles Darwin. (A close look at the skeletons of a small dinosaur and a bird reveals that they have many features in common.) One in-between fossil was discovered in Germany in 1860. It was an imprint of a crow-sized creature, beautifully preserved in limestone. Named *Archaeopteryx* ("ancient wing"), it looked mostly like a small dinosaur, with jaws, teeth, claws, and a long, bony tail. However, *Archaeopteryx* also had large feathers on its wings and tail, and hind toes that could have helped it perch in trees.

During most of the next century and a half, more fossils of *Archaeopteryx* were found (so far, a total of ten) but nothing of later evolutionary stages, closer to birds. Then, beginning in the

The tenth fossil skeleton discovered so far of Archaeopteryx, *a small, partly feathered dinosaur.*

mid-1990s, many fossils of small, feathered dinosaurs were uncovered in China. Some had lived at least ten million years after *Archaeopteryx*. Some had feathers covering their whole bodies. And, compared with *Archaeopteryx*, their heads and skeletons were less like reptiles, more like birds. Just as evolutionary scientists had predicted, the fossils showed that modern birds had evolved from dinosaurs.

Paleontologists continue to search for ancient bird relatives in rocks that formed about 100 to 120 million years ago. They are confident that such fossils will be found. Meanwhile, remember the idea that answering one question often leads to new questions? Well, discovery of *Archaeopteryx* and other links between dinosaurs and birds leads to this question: how did bird flight evolve?

Did these creatures run along the ground on their rear legs with outstretched front legs, and leap up to catch prey? (The individuals best at this would be better fed and more likely to pass on their characteristics to their offspring.) Or did they climb trees and glide down from them? (Individuals best at this might find plentiful food in trees and easily escape enemies. They, too, would be more likely to pass their characteristics on to a new generation.) Either way, feathered front legs (wings) would help. Either way, natural selection could favor those individuals that were best in the air. Natural selection would lead feathered dinosaurs to evolve into birds.

Much earlier, before dinosaurs roamed the land, there was another giant step in evolution: from fishes to land animals. Scientists found fish fossils with the beginnings of limbs, but nothing much further along. Beginning in 2000, a team of paleontologists began searching rock layers on Ellesmere Island in the Canadian Arctic. They picked the place on purpose. The sedimentary rocks, including siltstone, formed 375 million years ago. Judging from fossils found before and after that time, this was the period when fish evolved into land animals.

During the first few expeditions, little was found: a snout, parts of a jaw. Then, in 2004, three nearly complete skeletons were collected.

On cold, bleak Ellesmere Island, paleontologists uncovered fossil skeletons of the "fishapod" Tiktaalik *in the summer of 2004.*

The scientists had found an extraordinary "missing link"—*Tiktaalik* (pronounced tic-TAH-lick, the name means "big freshwater fish" in Inuit). Some call it "fishapod," because it had evolved in the direction of tetrapods, the first land animals. (*Tetrapod* is Greek for "four feet.")

Tiktaalik was still a fish, a scaly, finned predator that grew from four to nine feet long. However, it had a broad, flat head with eyes on top. It had a flexible neck. (Modern fish do not have necks.) It had strong-enough bones in its body and front fins that it could support itself in shallow water or on land. It probably did part of its breathing through lungs. And its fins were better for standing and crawling than for swimming. *Tiktaalik's* front pair of fins had simple wrist and fingerlike bones. It was a pioneer, well along in the evolution from swimming fish to crawling land animal.

Fifty million years ago, there was another remarkable series of changes in Earth's life: a land-dwelling mammal evolved into ocean-swimming whales. There is no doubt that whales evolved from land mammals. In fact, some whales still have rear leg bones in their bodies. Sometimes a baby whale is born with a rear leg—with feet and toes—sticking outside its body. (This means that whales still have some DNA directions for making limbs.)

Though fishlike in some ways, Tiktaalik *had a neck and limb bones that would enable it to crawl in shallow water or on land.*

On display at the University of Chicago, a model of Tiktaalik *alongside a* Tiktaalik *fossil skull and skeleton.*

Within the past twenty years, several whale "missing link" fossils have been discovered. One was found in rocks that formed fifty-two million years ago; another in fifty-million-year-old rocks; another in forty-seven-million-year-old rocks. In that order, each fossil mammal became more like a whale, with nostrils moving, over time, from the front to the top of the head and rear legs getting smaller and smaller. Paleontologists looked for fossils in younger rocks that formed forty million years ago and eventually found a whalelike creature called *Dorudon*. It had a nostril (blowhole) on top of its skull. *Dorudon* measured 50 feet (15 meters) long. It had short rear legs, but they were probably useless for such a large mammal. *Dorudon* almost certainly lived in water full-time, like a whale.

Evolution continued, and fossils of true whales (like those living today) were found in rocks that formed thirty million years ago.

Notice that scientists predicted the discovery of "missing links"—between dinosaurs and birds, between fishes and land animals, and between land animals and whales. Also, knowing the ages of rock layers, they can narrow their search for fossils of "missing links."

A prediction is a kind of test. The science of evolution keeps passing these tests. Scientists predict with confidence that more fossils will be found that show different stages when one form of life evolved into another.

Ancestors of whales had fully functioning hips and legs. In whales today (a humpback, left), all that remains are small, useless bones. Such limbs or organs are called *vestigial*. Other examples are found in caves where some species of fish and salamanders have little or no vision. These animals evolved from ancestors that had well-developed eyes, but vision was not needed in a pitch-black environment. Not all vestiges are useless. Flightless birds evolved from birds that could fly. Their wings can still be useful—but in a different way. Penguins' wings, for example, have evolved into flippers that make these birds speedy swimmers.

16

Moving Continents

Just as people used to believe that no animals had ever gone extinct, they thought that Earth's continents had never budged. This belief lasted a long time despite some intriguing discoveries. Geologists noticed that some layers of rocks along the western edge of Africa matched strata on parts of eastern South America. And the edges of those two continents looked like they might fit together, like pieces of a jigsaw puzzle. (Have a look at a world map.) Paleontologists also found similar fossils in those far-apart rock layers. But the idea of continents moving seemed preposterous—until new ideas, and plenty of evidence, led to the theory of continental drift and the theory of *plate tectonics*. (*Tekton* means "builder" in Greek.)

Geologists now believe that Earth's crust is made of about sixteen gigantic slabs, or plates, that rest on partly molten rock. The plates carry entire continents and ocean basins, and they do indeed move, at the speed of a half-inch to six inches (one to fifteen centimeters) a year. Some plates pull away from one another, and others collide. The Indian plate, pushing against the Eurasian plate, causes earthquakes in China and the continuing rise of the Himalaya Mountains.

At times in Earth's history, all of the land was present as a single giant continent. Most recently—about 200 million years ago—it was Pangaea ("all the land" in Greek). Now the continents are far apart, but geologists predict they will someday merge again. One thing is certain: all of these past changes had great effects on how life was, and is, spread around Earth. The study of the distribution of life on our planet, and how it got that way, is called *biogeography*.

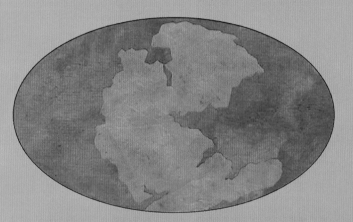

225 Million Years Ago

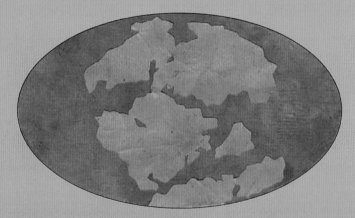

135 Million Years Ago

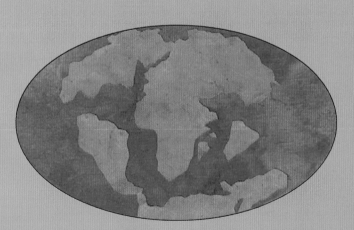

65 Million Years Ago

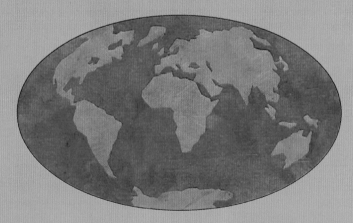

Present Time

Charles Darwin, inspired by his worldwide voyage of exploration, was one of the first scientists to ponder biogeography. Of course he had no idea that continents had been joined and torn apart over Earth's history. But he observed and wondered about animals and plants he found in different places. Since Darwin's time, scientists have learned a lot about how evolution is affected by geography.

One example is how a large group of mammals, called *marsupials*, came to be concentrated in one place, Australia. Marsupials include kangaroos, koalas, wallabies, wombats, and sugar gliders. When marsupials give birth, their tiny young crawl into a pouch. They nurse on milk and grow there. In this way, marsupials are quite different from other mammals, which give birth to young that are more fully developed and do not nurse inside a pouch. Native land mammals of Australia include more than 140 marsupial species and just two types of nonmarsupials, bats and rats.

People used to wonder why only Australia has a great variety of marsupials. Part of the answer comes from a long trail of fossils, part from knowing how Earth's land masses have moved, and part from understanding how life evolves.

North America has just one marsupial, a species of opossum. Yet, judging from fossils found in rock layers eighty million years old, marsupials first evolved in North America. (Marsupial teeth and jaws differ from those of other mammals, so their fossils can be identified with accuracy.) Fossils of marsupials have also been found near the tip of South America in forty-million-year-old rocks. And, in the early 1980s, scientists found fossils of a dozen species of marsupials in Antarctica. They lived there about thirty-five million years ago, about the time that marsupials reached Australia.

You may wonder: how did marsupials get across the water from

Earth's land masses, and oceans, are slowly on the move. Understanding these changes helps scientists explain why animal and plant species live in some places but not others.

In both appearance and behavior, marsupial sugar gliders (right) and flying squirrels (above) are quite similar, yet they evolved far apart, in Australia and North America.

South America to Antarctica, and from Antarctica to Australia? The answer: when they made this journey, there was no water to cross. These land masses were then connected. The Atlantic Ocean had not yet formed. Eventually, Australia was cut off from other land. It became a separate continent, home to an unknown number of marsupial species but to very few other mammals.

Marsupials had a whole continent, with a variety of habitats, on which to evolve.

There were plenty of opportunities for them to adapt to new environments. So today Australia has an amazing variety of marsupial species (plus others that went extinct). Aside from being marsupials, some are remarkably like unrelated mammals found elsewhere. There are marsupial moles, anteaters, mice, sloths, and cats. The marsupial sugar glider looks and behaves remarkably like the flying squirrel of North America. Wombats are like groundhogs. The Tasmanian wolf, an extinct marsupial, was a predator like wolves of Europe and North America.

The remarkable similarity of some Australian mammals to unrelated mammals that live elsewhere is an example of what biologists call *convergent evolution*. (*Converge* means to "tend toward a common conclusion or result.") Australia's marsupials are just one example of how living things in far distant places can evolve in similar ways. Here are some other examples of convergent evolution, in both animals and plants:

Adapting to desert habitats, plants have evolved in ways to save water. They have small leaves (or no leaves) and fleshy stems that store water. You can see plants like this in deserts all over the world. However, they are not all close relatives. Cacti evolved in North and South America. Plants called euphorbs evolved in Asia, Africa, and Australia.

Cacti and euphorbs can be told apart by their flowers and their sap. However, by evolving to live in deserts, these two different plant groups are amazingly alike.

Birds and insects are certainly not closely related, yet there are hummingbirds and hummingbird moths. They both hover in the air while sipping nectar from flowers. By becoming adapted to that food source, their evolution caused them to look and fly alike.

A cactus species of Arizona (left) looks remarkably like a euphorb species of South Africa (right). Adapting to desert habitats, both evolved similar characteristics.

All ant-eating mammals are strikingly alike in some ways. Ants are abundant but tiny, so mammals that rely on ants as food must have a long sticky tongue to slurp up hundreds at once. They also need large salivary glands. Extra saliva helps keep their tongues sticky and washes ants down. Teeth aren't needed, but long snouts and powerful claws for digging are. All of these characteristics are found in the spiny anteater of Australia, the giant anteater of South America, and the pangolin of Africa. They aren't close relatives, and they live on different continents. Once again, the process of convergent evolution led them to have very similar traits.

Adapting to a diet of ants led mammals on different continents to evolve similar traits. Shown at right: the spiny anteater of Australia (top), giant anteater of South America (center), and pangolin of Africa (bottom).

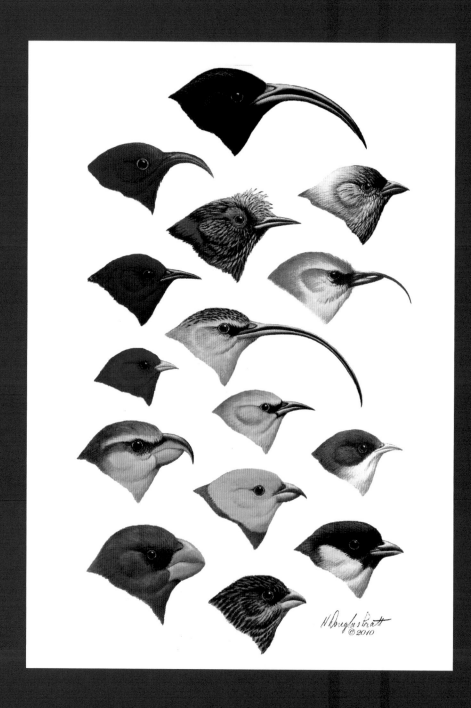

17

On Faraway Islands

Ever since the Galápagos Islands sparked plenty of ideas and questions in Charles Darwin, scientists who study biogeography have been fascinated by island life. Unusual species of animals and plants evolve on islands—particularly those that are farthest from the continents.

Madagascar was once part of Africa, but about 160 million years ago it moved farther and farther into the Indian Ocean. It became home to a great variety of new species that were found nowhere else on Earth. Seventy-five species of lemurs lived there (before humans caused the extinction of many kinds). One group of birds, called vangas, reminds scientists of the Galápagos finches. They evolved traits like those of birds on faraway continents (another example of convergent evolution). The twenty-two species of vangas include birds like woodpeckers, nuthatches, flycatchers, tree creepers, and predatory shrikes. Vangas exist only on Madagascar.

Far to the east of Madagascar, in the middle of the Pacific, lie the Hawaiian Islands. Created by volcanoes, they have never been part of a continent. These islands have no native reptiles, amphibians, land mammals, or freshwater fish. Without human help, such animals have very little chance of ever reaching faraway islands.

Birds have a much better chance, since they can fly and can be

The amazing diversity of Hawaiian honeycreepers is shown in this painting by H. Douglas Pratt. They include species that feed on flower nectar, seeds, or insects. All evolved from one finch species that reached the Hawaiian Islands four million years ago.

carried far by hurricanes or other great storms. Scientists believe that a species of finch reached Hawaii about four million years ago. Over time that one species evolved into nearly sixty different kinds of birds called honeycreepers. Like Galápagos finches, Hawaiian honeycreepers have a great variety of beaks. Some are adapted for eating certain sizes of seeds or fruits or for catching insects. One honeycreeper called the Maui parrotbill has a big, hooked beak. It rips bark off tree trunks and splits twigs to find beetle larvae.

The amazing variety of Hawaiian honeycreepers, of Galápagos finches, of the vangas of Madagascar—are all examples of *adaptive radiation*. In each case, one species of bird somehow reached an

Lifeless at first, isolated volcanic islands are gradually populated by plants and animals that evolve to adapt to new habitats.

Hawaiian plants called silverswords are another example of adaptive radiation. Genetic research reveals that these plants are related to tarweeds that grow on the west coast of North America. Tarweeds have sticky fruits. Scientists believe that some tarweed seeds—stuck to bird feathers—were accidentally carried to the Hawaiian Islands several million years ago. From the original tarweed, twenty-eight species of silverswords have evolved. They vary greatly in their looks, ways of growing, and habitats. Some grow in lowland bogs, others on high altitude volcanic cinder cones. The photograph shows a Haleakala silversword on Maui's highest peak, Haleakala.

isolated island. There was little competition, few predators, and a whole new island world. This was a great opportunity to spread, or radiate, into new habitats, adapting through evolution into many different species. That is why oceanic islands and archipelagoes have amazing groups of related species that all do different things.

18

Coevolution

Orchids fascinated Charles Darwin. He carefully cut apart their complex blossoms to understand their structure. He watched flying insects visit orchid flowers, seeking nectar. He learned that the structure of each kind of orchid ensured that flower pollen stuck to the bodies of visiting insects. The insects then carried pollen to other orchid flowers of the same species, making it possible for the orchids to produce seeds. Insects, bats, and birds that transfer pollen in this way are called *pollinators*.

Botanists sent orchid plants from all over the world to Darwin. One of the most remarkable came from Madagascar. Examining its flowers, Darwin found that nectar was stored at the bottom of an 11-inch (28-centimeter) tube. He wrote that the orchid must have an unusual pollinator—a species of moth with very long *proboscis* (a narrow tube that uncoils and serves as a straw, for sipping nectar). Darwin's prediction was correct. Forty years later the moth was found in Madagascar. Now called Darwin's hawk moth, it

Darwin's hawk moth, with its exceptionally long proboscis.

has a proboscis that measures between 12 and 14 inches (30 and 35 centimeters).

Other kinds of insects may try to reach the orchid's nectar, but just one kind of moth succeeds. The orchid and the moth are perfectly adapted to each other. Their mutual adaptation is called *coevolution*. Among flowering plants and their pollinators there are many examples of coevolution. Some kinds of flowers have evolved in other ways that attract bees as pollinators. Bees can see ultraviolet light. Flowers have evolved patterns, visible in ultraviolet, that help bees get to their nectar (and to pollen that the bees spread to other flowers). The patterns are called *nectar guides*. (They aren't visible to human eyes, unless the flowers are photographed using a special light filter.)

Bats are important pollinators. Many trees and shrubs in the tropics may have coevolved with bats that feed on nectar. North America has eleven species of nectar-feeding bats. (Note: not every match of plant and pollinator is an example of coevolution, in which both have evolved together and in response to each other.) In Mexico and the southwestern United States, long-nosed bats are vital pollinators of saguaro and organ-pipe cactus flowers. The showy white blossoms gleam in the darkness. The bats have long noses and tongues that enable them to reach the nectar in the flowers.

Natural selection produces evolutionary changes that help living things become better adapted to thrive in their environments. Flowers and their pollinators have benefited from evolving in a kind

of partnership. However, coevolution can also be part of an "arms race" between predator and prey.

Moths are food for many insect-eating bats. When these bats send out high-pitched sounds and receive the echoes, they can pinpoint a flying moth. (This is called an *echolocation* system.) As a bat zeroes in on its prey, it emits more and more sounds toward its target. Some species of moths have evolved defenses. They are able to detect sounds, especially the high-pitched sounds that bats emit.

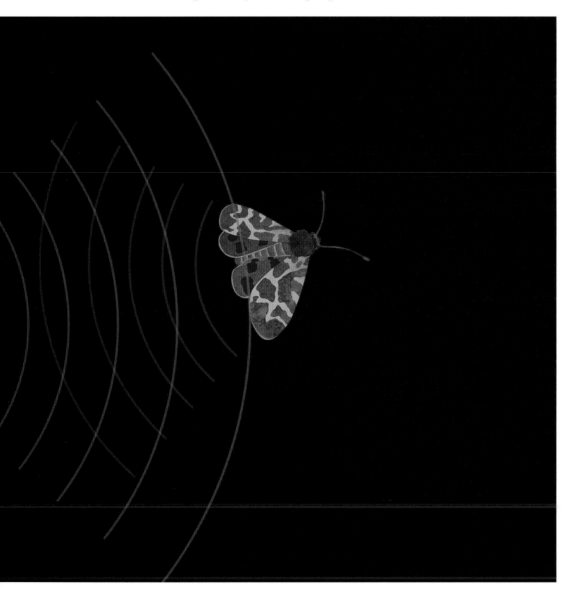

High-pitched sounds from a bat bounce off objects and return as echoes the bat can hear. This echolocation system enables bats to catch flying insects.

The pronghorn is North America's fastest mammal.

Animals that have lived on islands without predators are usually defenseless when predatory animals invade the islands later, usually when brought by humans. Normally, predator and prey animals evolve together, and this causes evolutionary changes in their bodies, senses, and behavior. This is what poet Robinson Jeffers meant when he wrote:

> What but the wolf's tooth whittled so fine
> the fleet limbs of the antelope?

Scientists have wondered why the American pronghorn is so swift. Pronghorns can run forty-five miles an hour for several miles, with bursts of nearly sixty miles an hour. They easily escape from coyotes and wolves—the fastest predators now in their lives—and their extra speed seems to be unnecessary. It's probably a remnant of their evolutionary past. More than ten thousand years ago, pronghorns were chased by much speedier predators: the North American cheetah and a species of long-legged hyena. Today the pronghorn is probably amazingly fast because it evolved with swift predators that are now extinct.

The moths have also evolved another defense: when they detect bats' calls, they zig-zag, loop, or dive to escape. Tiger moths have evolved an even better defense. They make clicking sounds that seem to confuse bats' echolocation systems.

Tiger moths now have an edge in the arms race with their enemies. However, it may be a temporary advantage. Both bats and moths continue to evolve. In this coevolution of predator and prey, bats may eventually change and somehow overcome the defense of tiger moths.

19

Origin of Species

The word *species* has already been used many times in this book. People have a general idea of its meaning. They understand that robins and cardinals are two separate bird species. They know that ravens and crows are also distinct species, though they are close relatives.

Most scientists define a species as a group of interbreeding natural populations that do not interbreed with other groups. In other words, a group of animals or plants is considered a species when its members can't successfully breed with other groups. Robins do not mate with cardinals, nor do crows mate with ravens. Species of plants also do not interbreed. If a bee accidentally leaves pollen from a snapdragon flower within a hollyhock blossom, the pollen has no effect. No seeds form, though it is fun to imagine snaphock or hollydragon plants. Donkeys can mate with horses, and even produce offspring, but those offspring, called mules, are sterile and cannot reproduce. Donkeys and horses are thus considered members of different species.

Earth is home to millions of different species—not to mention many other millions that have gone extinct. How do animals and plants become separate species?

Sometimes new species evolve when some individuals of a species become physically separated from the rest of their population. The chapter "On Faraway Islands" (on pages 70–73) gives dramatic examples of birds that reached isolated islands and radiated by evolution into many different species.

Caribbean Sea

Isthmus of Panama

Pacific Ocean

It is easy to imagine the geographic isolation of islands in oceans. However, living things on continents, or in one state, or in a smaller area, can also be cut off from others of their kind. The barrier can be a rising mountain range or a river. In the Amazon Basin of South America, river channels have changed countless times over millions of years. In this ever-changing landscape, parts of populations are isolated. There have been, and still are, many opportunities for new species to evolve in the Amazon Basin.

According to experts on plate tectonics, North America and South America have been connected then disconnected and reconnected repeatedly over many millions of years. The most recent reconnection occurred about three million years ago. Then a land bridge, the Isthmus of Panama, rose. (Four different tectonic plates are involved, so the geology of the area is very complex.) The land bridge created a barrier in the water where none had been before. Populations of sea creatures were separated, some on the Pacific Ocean side, some on the Atlantic Ocean side. Because of the barrier, the shallow-water environment of each side changed. New species began to evolve. Today there are seven species of snapping shrimp on the Pacific side, and seven different species of snapping

When tectonic plates pushed the Isthmus of Panama above water, the new land barrier affected evolution of sea life in the Caribbean Sea (top) and the Pacific Ocean.

shrimp on the Atlantic side. Each species has its closest relative on the other side of the isthmus.

In a New Mexico desert, a dramatic change in the environment is producing new species of rodents, lizards, and insects. When a salty lake dried up about seven thousand years ago, huge amounts of gypsum sand remained. Winds created 275 square miles (712 square kilometers) of white sand dunes. The mostly brown color of small desert animals made them stand out against the white sand. Predators could easily spot them.

The individual lizards and other animals that were palest in color were more likely to escape predators and live to produce the next generation. Over a few thousand years, natural selection has produced seven new species with white coloration, all from darker-colored ancestors. They are three species of lizards, two of camel crickets, a pocket mouse, and a wood rat. All of them blend in well among the white dunes.

Brown lizards live in the desert habitat surrounding the dunes, but the brown lizards and the white lizards do not seem to interbreed. This is evidence that they are now separate species.

The new dune habitat of White Sands, New Mexico, is causing animals to adapt and evolve into new species.

A lizard from the white sand dune habitat (left), and its close relative (right) from the nearby desert.

In case after case, new species evolve when a physical barrier or change in habitat separates parts of animal or plant populations. Over time the separated populations evolve in different ways. Two populations of birds, for example, might evolve to be quite distinct in some ways, perhaps in their colors, beak shapes, or courtship behaviors. Genetically, the populations would be quite different from each other. Even if the physical barrier between the two groups no longer existed, the bird populations would not interbreed and would not mix their genes. They would be separate species.

20

Evolution, Going On Right Now

When people think of evolution happening, they imagine a very slow process. Generally this is true. Some known evolutionary transitions—from fishes to land animals, for instance—took millions of years. Charles Darwin wrote, "We see nothing of these slow changes in progress." Evolution, he thought, could only be seen in a series of fossils, found in older, then younger, layers of rocks.

Today, Darwin would be delighted to see a fast-growing list of cases of evolution-in-action. Over 150 examples have been described by scientists so far. Evolution has been observed in laboratory studies and in the wild. In some cases, evolution occurred over a span of a few decades; in other cases, over just a few years or less. The variety of rapidly evolving life includes flowers, birds, reptiles, mammals; aphids, fruit flies, and other insects; and several kinds of fish, including salmon, guppies, and sticklebacks. Here are a few examples:

Hawaii's scarlet honeycreeper (which has the Hawaiian name *'I'iwi*) feeds mostly on flower nectar. When its main source of food, called *lobeloids*, began to disappear, this species turned to other flowers, and over a few decades its beak evolved to a shorter length.

When fire ants began spreading through the southeastern United States, they became a threat to fence lizards. Bites of just a dozen fire ants can kill a three-inch lizard. Biologists compared populations of fence lizards that lived near fire ants with lizards that did not. They

A scarlet honeycreeper ('I'iwi*) feeds on flower nectar.*

Thanks to natural variation among blue moon butterflies, their population evolved to "disarm" a deadly bacterium.

found that lizards threatened by fire ants are adapting—changing their behavior and their hind legs. They twitch their bodies to flick off ants. And, remarkably, the fence lizards are evolving longer back legs. This makes them more successful at fleeing from fire ants.

When deadly bacteria struck blue moon butterflies on two Samoan islands in the South Pacific, they killed males before they could hatch into caterpillars. Soon males were only one percent of the population. The blue moon butterflies were in danger of dying out. However, the surviving males had a "suppressor" gene that disarmed the bacteria. When they mated, this gene was passed on to the next generation, and the next. In just ten generations, males made up forty percent of blue moon butterflies. The butterflies were no longer in danger from the bacteria. (This took only about a year; tropical insects can breed year-round and have many generations in one year.)

On Daphne Major Island of the Galápagos, Peter and Rosemary Grant have studied finch evolution for more than thirty years.

Another example of evolution that occurred in a very short time took place on one of the Galápagos Islands. Charles Darwin spent just five weeks on these islands. Beginning in 1973, biologists Peter and Rosemary Grant (who are husband and wife) began annual studies at a small Galápagos island named Daphne Major.

More than thirty years of research have led to some startling discoveries. The climate of the Galápagos varies dramatically, from years of plentiful rain to those of severe drought. This affects plant growth and the seeds that are available for birds to eat. The Grants learned that drought years greatly reduced the abundance of small seeds.

This, in turn, affected the evolution of finches. Individuals of the medium ground finch were forced to eat bigger, harder seeds than the small

All living things evolve, humans included. The human species, *Homo sapiens* (Latin for "wise man"), is part of a group called primates. Genetic research shows that of all species, chimpanzees are genetically closest to humans. This does not mean that humans evolved from chimpanzees, gorillas, or other modern-day primates. No scientist believes that. According to genetic research, humans and other primates had a common ancestor about six million years ago. They have evolved separately ever since.

seeds they prefer. Smaller individuals could not crack the seeds and starved to death, while individuals with bigger beaks survived to mate and pass this trait to their young. Over many years of their research, the Grants have discovered that the beak size of finches can evolve from one year to the next as the climate swings from wet to dry and back again.

Visible, measurable evolution in one year—that is exciting news. However, equally fast—and even faster—evolution is going on. It does not involve appealing, colorful birds or fish or flowers. Quite the opposite—the organisms that can and do evolve very quickly are insect pests and germs that can harm or even kill humans. (The word *germs* means harmful bacteria, viruses, and other microscopic organisms. They are sometimes called *microbes*.)

In the 1940s, scientists discovered that the process of evolution helps insect pests defeat the pesticides meant to kill them. At first, a pesticide called DDT killed most mosquitoes and other insect pests. Some survived. They lived because there is genetic variation in mosquitoes, as there is in all animal populations. The survivors were immune to DDT. They lived to reproduce and pass their traits on to future generations. This form of natural selection eventually produced mosquito populations that were resistant to DDT.

A virus is the most simple form of life. In fact, a virus really comes to life only after it gets inside a cell of a living organism. There it can make thousands of copies of itself. Each new virus can invade other cells, and a viral infection can grow.

Each virus is only about one one-hundredth the size of a bacterium, but viruses still contain genes and evolve. Like all microbes, viruses can evolve so that they are resistant to antiviral drugs.

Evolution has also produced populations of houseflies and agricultural pests that were not harmed by pesticides. By 1990, more than five hundred insect pests (including 114 species of mosquitoes) had evolved resistance to at least one pesticide. One example is bedbugs, which were once well controlled by insecticides called pyrethroids. Then two mutations in a gene caused some bedbugs to be unharmed by pyrethroids. Now bedbugs are major pests in cities of the United States and Europe. Researchers are trying to find a new chemical weapon against them. However, because of variation among bedbugs, and because of evolution, any success is likely to be only temporary.

Each new generation is an opportunity for evolutionary change. It can happen quickly among insects because many species have several generations in just one year. Fruit flies, for example, can have a life cycle—egg to adult—in just ten days. However, fruit flies are slowpokes compared with bacteria, which can reproduce every twenty minutes. Also, bacteria and other germs have enormous populations. (A billion bacteria can be kept in a small laboratory flask.) With huge numbers and many new generations in a single day, there are also many mutations. Microbes can evolve quickly.

In the 1940s, the drug penicillin cured infections caused by bacteria called *Staphylococcus*. Now penicillin is ineffective against more than ninety-five percent of staph strains in the world. Some new antibiotic drugs work, though the bacteria will probably evolve resistance to them, too. (This does not always occur. It depends on the right mutations happening. So far the strain of *Streptococcus* bacteria that causes strep throat has not evolved resistance to antibiotics.)

The numbers of drug-resistant bacteria continue to increase. There are now cases in which doctors must remove a patient's wounded limb because no antibiotic drug can stop infection from spreading. Worldwide, one out of thirty cases of tuberculosis (a sometimes fatal lung disease) now resists treatment by antibiotics that used to be effective.

Mutations occur in flu viruses, sometimes producing worrisome new strains of flu. Early in this century, it was avian (bird) flu, caused by the H5N1 virus. It killed birds, but did not easily infect humans. Medical researchers still worry that a few mutations could enable a deadly flu virus to spread readily to people.

People worry about flu and other diseases that could cause sickness and death. When they do so, most people do not realize that they are thinking about evolution. Nevertheless, they are. Natural selection is the process that can cause a microbe to change into a potential threat to humans. Without meaning to, humans are helping this evolution along. Use of antibiotic drugs kills off vulnerable germs. This helps speed the evolution of drug-resistant germs.

Clearly, evolution is not just about changes in flowers and frogs. It can be a matter of life or death. Medical researchers are keenly aware of this. Their knowledge of genetics, including DNA studies of microbes, offers hope that ways can be found to defeat drug-resistant germs.

The field of medicine is just one kind of science in which understanding of evolution is vital. Knowledge about evolution is now the foundation of biology, paleontology, genetics, and other sciences. Many kinds of scientists continue to explore details of evolution. Their discoveries lead to new questions, and sometimes to disagreements. The questions and debates are eventually settled—by research, and by finding trustworthy evidence. That is how science is done.

In the years ahead, we will learn even more about evolution, about how it works, and about how it affects our lives. Meanwhile, we can marvel at some understandings gained in the past 150 years:

- the mind-boggling age of Earth—time enough for evolution to produce an amazing variety of life, now and in the past
- the story of Earth's life written in rock layers with the fossils they hold
- the evidence from DNA that ties all animals and plants together, from the primitive to the most complex, as having common ancestors
- the simple but powerful process of natural selection that causes change in living things and is also the origin of new species

It is exciting to think of new discoveries and to learn even more of the fascinating story of evolution.

Glossary

adaptation. A characteristic of an animal or plant that improves its chances of reproducing or surviving in its environment (for example, the ability of desert plants to store water).

adaptive radiation. The evolution of a variety of life that usually begins when one species reaches a new environment (for example, a Hawaiian island). From that one species others evolve as they adapt to a variety of habitats.

biogeography. The scientific study of how and why living things are distributed as they are on Earth.

botany. The scientific study of plants.

coevolution. The joint evolution of different, unrelated organisms whose adaptations have important effects on one another. One example: a moth and an orchid that are perfectly adapted so that just that one moth species can pollinate the orchid species' flowers.

convergent evolution. The process by which different animals or plants, not closely related, evolve similar characteristics that enable them to thrive in similar habitats, even if those habitats are far away from each other. One example: Australian sugar gliders and North American flying squirrels.

deoxyribonucleic acid. See DNA.

DNA. An abbreviation for *deoxyribonucleic acid*. The molecule in cells of living things that contains their genetic information.

double helix. A pair of twisting strands. The term describes the structure of DNA.

echolocation. A sensing system in many species of bats, as well as in toothed whales, dolphins, and cave-dwelling birds. Animals emit calls and listen to the echoes, using the information to navigate and to locate and catch prey.

erosion. The wearing away of soil, rocks, and other substances, mostly by flowing water but also by wind.

evo-devo. An abbreviation for *evolutionary developmental biology*. The combined study of evolution and development (for example, how evolution has produced the changes that occur as a mature plant develops from a seed).

evolution. A process by which the genetic characteristics of a population or an entire species of organisms changes, usually over a long period of time.

extinction. A process by which all individuals of a species die out, so that the species no longer exists. Most species that ever existed in Earth's long history (more than 99 percent of them) became extinct without leaving descendants.

fossils. Skeletons, tracks, and other traces of animals or plants from past ages that are preserved, usually in rocks. Fossils also include ants and other insects trapped in tree resin that eventually changed to hard amber.

genes. Parts of DNA molecules that contain chemical "directions" that determine the characteristics of the individuals of a new generation.

genetics. The study of the heredity of living things, or how the characteristics of one generation are passed to generations that follow.

genome. The complete genetic information present in the cells of an organism.

geology. The scientific study of the history and structure of Earth.

habitat. The place or environment where an organism normally lives. For example, the Antarctic coast is the habitat of Adelie penguins.

half-life. The time needed for half of a sample of a radioactive element to break down, or decay, into another element. For example, the half-life of lead-214 is 27 minutes, while that of plutonium-239 is 24,000 years.

igneous rocks. Types of rocks that form from lava and other molten materials, such as those produced by volcanoes.

marsupials. Mammals whose young are sheltered and nursed inside a pouch on the mother's belly.

microbes. Microscopic forms of life, such as bacteria and viruses.

mutation. A change in the genetic material of a cell that can result in offspring that are somewhat different from parents.

natural selection. A process in nature through which organisms best adapted to their environments tend to survive and reproduce, passing their characteristics on to a new generation. This process is the basic driving force in the evolution of life.

nectar guides. Patterns on flowers that are visible to bees and some other insects, guiding the insects to nectar. These patterns help the process of pollination as insects accidentally carry pollen from blossom to blossom.

nucleus. The center of an animal or plant cell, which contains the genetic information of that individual organism.

ornithology. The scientific study of birds.

paleontology. The scientific study of prehistoric life, including fossils formed from long-extinct animals.

plate tectonics. A scientific theory that explains how movements of huge plates that form Earth's crust not only move the continents around, but also cause earthquakes, volcanic eruptions, continental drift, and mountain building.

pollination. In plants that reproduce by means of flowers, the process by which pollen from one flower part is transferred to another flower. (Pollen grains contain the male sex cells of flowers.) Moths and other insects play a vital role in spreading pollen from flower to flower and are called pollinators.

radioactivity. Behavior of a substance in which the atomic nucleus of an unstable atom loses energy by emitting particles. Radioactivity occurs naturally in about fifty elements, such as radium and uranium. The process of losing energy and particles is called radioactive decay.

sedimentary rocks. Types of rocks that gradually form from such sediments as mud, silt, and sand that settle to the bottoms of oceans, lakes, and other natural basins. Common sedimentary rocks are siltstone, shale, and sandstone.

species. A population or many populations of an organism that have characteristics that make them different from other populations and unable to exchange genes with them.

toolkit genes. Genes that control the development of organs, limbs, and other parts of an organism.

trait. A characteristic, such as eye color, that is inherited from past generations.

vestige. The remnant of an animal organ or limb that was fully developed and useful in past generations, then evolved to become practically useless (for example, whale legs) or useful in a different way (for example, penguin flippers).

virus. A simple, microscopic form of life that is unable to reproduce without being inside cells of a living organism.

To Learn More

BOOKS

Gamlin, Linda. *Evolution*. London: Dorling Kindersley, 2009.

Jenkins, Steve. *Life on Earth: The Story of Evolution*. Boston: Houghton Mifflin, 2002.

Lawson, Kristan. *Darwin and Evolution for Kids*. Chicago: Chicago Review Press, 2003.

McNulty, Faith. *How Whales Walked into the Sea*. New York: Scholastic Press, 1999.

Nardo, Don. *The Theory of Evolution: A History of Life on Earth*. Minneapolis: Compass Point Books, 2010.

Peters, Lisa Westberg. *Our Family Tree: An Evolution Story*. San Diego: Harcourt, 2003.

Sis, Peter. *The Tree of Life: A Book Depicting the Life of Charles Darwin, Naturalist, Geologist & Thinker*. New York: Farrar Straus Giroux, 2003.

Sloan, Christopher. *The Human Story: Our Evolution from Prehistoric Ancestors to Today*. Washington, DC: National Geographic, 2004.

Webster, Stephen. *The Kingfisher Book of Evolution*. New York: Kingfisher, 2000.

Winston, Robert. *Evolution Revolution*. New York: DK Publishing, 2009.

WEBSITES*

EVOLUTION RESOURCES

Public Broadcasting Service
pbs.org/wgbh/evolution
Click on "Evolution Library" or "for Students."

EVOLUTION EDUCATION

EvoEdu: Evolution Education
evoedu.com
Understanding Evolution
University of California Museum of Paleontology
evolution.berkeley.edu

EVOLUTION NEWS

The sites below report scientific discoveries, which sometimes include fossils, DNA research findings, and other exciting news about evolution.
sciencenewsforkids.org
amnh.org/ology

*Active at time of publication

Sources

BOOKS

Carroll, Sean B. *Endless Forms Most Beautiful: The New Science of Evo Devo and the Making of the Animal Kingdom*. New York: W. W. Norton, 2005.

Carroll, Sean B. *Remarkable Creatures: Epic Adventures in the Search for the Origins of Species*. Boston: Houghton Mifflin Harcourt, 2009.

Chiappe, Luis M. *Glorified Dinosaurs: The Origin and Early Evolution of Birds*. Hoboken, NJ: John Wiley & Sons, 2007.

Coyne, Jerry A. *Why Evolution Is True*. New York: Viking, 2009.

Darwin, Charles. *The Origin of Species*. New York: Random House, 1979.

Lane, Nick. *Life Ascending: The Ten Great Inventions of Evolution*. New York: W. W. Norton, 2009.

Liebes, Sidney, Elisabet Sahtouris, and Brian Swimme. *A Walk Through Time: From Stardust to Us.* New York: John Wiley & Sons, 1998.

Pojeta, John, and Dale Springer. *Evolution and the Fossil Record.* Alexandria, VA: American Geological Institute, 2001.

Prothero, Donald R. *Evolution: What the Fossils Say and Why It Matters.* New York: Columbia University Press, 2007.

Quammen, David. *The Reluctant Mr. Darwin: An Intimate Portrait of Charles Darwin and the Making of His Theory of Evolution.* New York: W. W. Norton, 2006.

Quammen, David. *The Song of the Dodo: Island Biogeography in an Age of Extinctions.* New York: Scribner, 1996.

Ruse, Michael. *Defining Darwin: Essays on the History and Philosophy of Evolutionary Biology.* Amherst, NY: Prometheus Books, 2009.

Ruse, Michael, and Joseph Travis, editors. *Evolution: The First Four Billion Years.* Cambridge, MA: Harvard University Press, 2009.

Shubin, Neil. *Your Inner Fish: A Journey into the 3.5-Billion-Year History of the Human Body.* New York: Pantheon, 2008.

Turney, Chris. *Bones, Rocks, and Stars: The Science of When Things Happened.* New York: Macmillan, 2006.

Zimmer, Carl. *Evolution: The Triumph of an Idea.* New York: HarperCollins, 2001.

PERIODICALS

Carroll, Sean B. "The Origins of Form." *Natural History*, November 2005, 58–63.

Conrod, William. "A Desert Galapagos." *Natural History*, May 2008, 16–18.

Marsa, Linda. "Galapagos Next: Six Evolutionary Hot Spots Are Testing and Extending Darwin's Discoveries in Startling Ways." *Discover*, March 2009, 46–49.

Miller, Lee, and Annemarie Surlykke. "How Some Insects Detect and Avoid Being Eating by Bats: Tactics and Countertactics of Prey and Predator." *Bioscience*, July 2001, 570–581.

Prothero, Donald. "The Fossils Say Yes: The Discovery of Transitional Forms Has Filled in Some of the Most Talked-About Gaps in the Fossil Record." *Natural History*, November 2005, 52–56.

Quammen, David. "Darwin's First Clues." *National Geographic*, February 2009, 44–55.

Quammen, David. "The Man Who Wasn't Darwin." *National Geographic*, December 2008, 106–133.

Quammen, David. "Was Darwin Wrong?" *National Geographic*, November 2004, 3–35.

Ridley, Matt. "Modern Darwins." *National Geographic*, February 2009, 56–73.

Schwartz, Douglas W. "An Evolving Genius: The Extraordinary Early Life of Charles Darwin." *Anthronotes*, Fall 2008, 1–9.

Wade, Nicholas. "Finch DNA Shows Darwin Was Right." *New York Times*, May 11, 1999, F5.

Weiner, Jonathan. "Evolution in Action." *Natural History*, November 2005, 47–51.

Wilford, John Noble. "Flute Music Wafted in Caves 35,000 Years Ago." *New York Times*, June 25, 2009, A12.

Zimmer, Carl. "A Fin Is a Limb Is a Wing." *National Geographic*, November 2006, 111–135.

Image Credits

Note
The family photos opposite page 11 are: top, two of the author's children, Rebecca and Jesse, in the early 1990s; middle left, the author's brother, Gary, with Laurence on tricycle; middle right, the author in school photo, perhaps fourth grade; bottom left, unidentified relative of late 1800s–early 1900s; bottom right, the author on mother Marleah's lap, Gary on right, 1936. Also, the author's daughter Heidi is shown on page 17.

Index

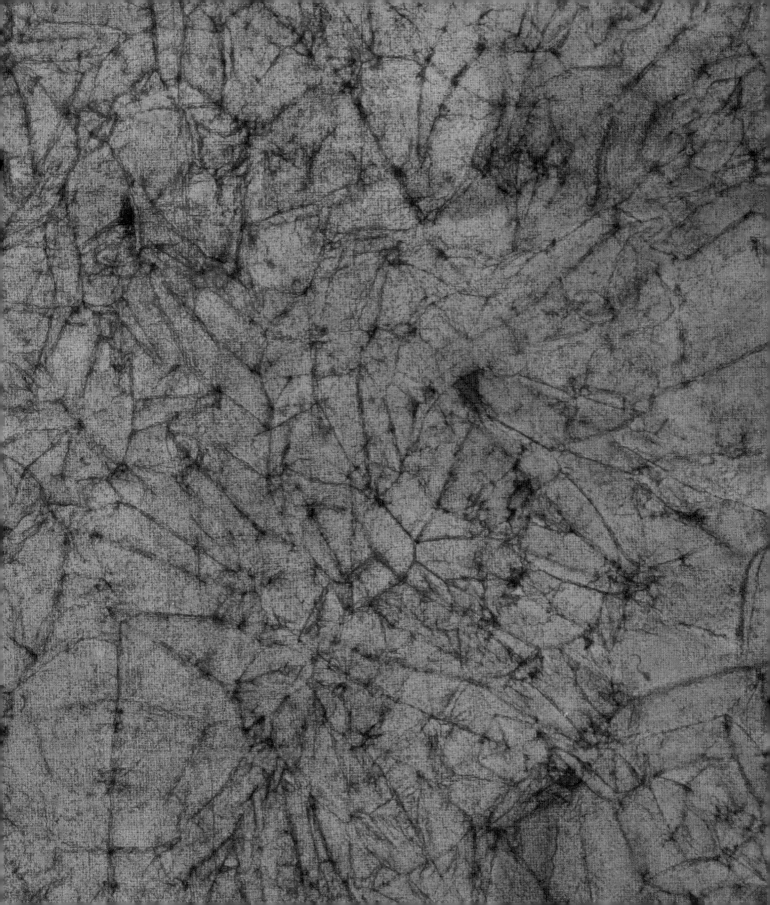

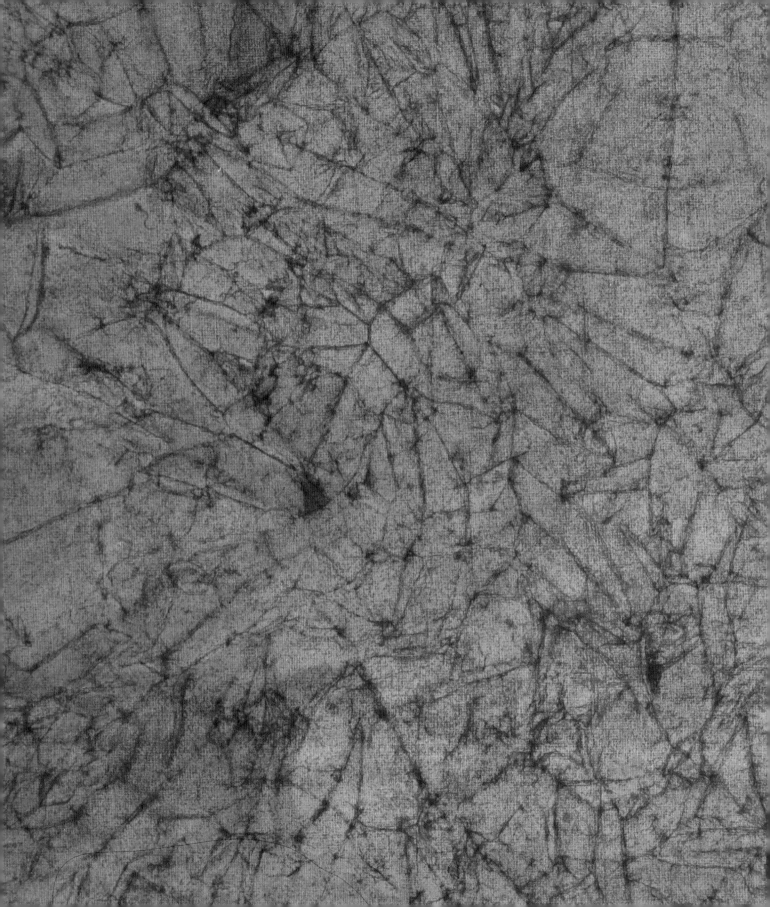